WORLD ALMANAC® LIBRARY

OF THE

AMERICAN REVOLUTION

The Patriots Win
the American Revolution

Dale Anderson

🌐 WORLD ALMANAC® LIBRARY

Please visit our web site at: www.worldalmanaclibrary.com
For a free color catalog describing World Almanac® Library's list of high-quality books
and multimedia programs, call 1-800-848-2928 (USA) or 1-800-387-3178 (Canada).
World Almanac® Library's fax: (414) 332-3567.

Library of Congress Cataloging-in-Publication Data

Anderson, Dale, 1953-
    The patriots win the American Revolution / by Dale Anderson.
        p. cm. — (World Almanac Library of the American Revolution)
    Includes bibliographical references and index.
    ISBN 0-8368-5928-6 (lib. bdg.)
    ISBN 0-8368-5937-5 (softcover)
    1. United States—History—Revolution, 1775-1783—Campaigns—Juvenile literature. 2. United States—
History—Revolution, 1775-1783—British Forces—Juvenile literature. 3. United States—History—Revolution,
1775-1783—Biography—Juvenile literature. 4. Generals—United States—Biography—Juvenile literature.
5. Generals—Great Britain—Biography—Juvenile literature. I. Title. II. Series.
    E230.A54   2005
    973.3'3—dc22   2005040811

First published in 2006 by
World Almanac® Library
A Member of the WRC Media Family of Companies
330 West Olive Street, Suite 100
Milwaukee, WI 53212 USA

Produced by Discovery Books
Editor: Sabrina Crewe
Designer and page production: Sabine Beaupré
Photo researcher: Sabrina Crewe
Maps and diagrams: Stefan Chabluk
Consultant: Andrew Frank, Assistant Professor of History, Florida Atlantic University
World Almanac® Library editorial direction: Mark J. Sachner
World Almanac® Library editor: Alan Wachtel
World Almanac® Library art direction: Tammy West
World Almanac® Library production: Jessica Morris

Photo credits: CORBIS: pp. 9, 33 (top), 37; The Granger Collection: pp. 8, 27, 38; Independence National Historical Park:
title page, pp. 14, 19, 29, 31; Library of Congress: cover, pp. 20, 24, 35; National Archives: pp. 5, 41; National Park Service:
pp. 15, 25; North Wind Picture Archives: pp. 12, 17, 34.

Printed in Canada

1 2 3 4 5 6 7 8 9 09 08 07 06 05

*Front cover: In 1783, after Britain formally recognized the United States of America in the Treaty of Paris, the last British
troops finally left the former colonies. On November 25, 1783, George Washington (on white horse) and his army made
a triumphant entry into New York City.*

*Title page: James Peale painted this portrait of George Washington on horseback in about 1790. He based the
portrait on a work by his brother, Charles Willson Peale—the faces of both the brothers can be seen on the left,
behind Washington. In the background on the right are Revolutionary soldiers, one carrying a French flag.*

Contents

I n 1776, the thirteen British **colonies** along the eastern coast of North America declared themselves independent of Britain. The colonists were already fighting British soldiers in protest at British policies. In 1781, the British surrendered to American forces, and, in 1783, they formally recognized the colonies' independence.

A New Nation

The movement from colonies to independence, known as the American Revolution, gave birth to a new nation—the United States of America. Eventually, the nation stretched to the Pacific Ocean and grew to comprise fifty states. Over time, it was transformed from a nation of farmers into an industrial and technological giant, the world's richest and most powerful country.

An Inspiration to Others

The American Revolution was based on a revolution of ideas. The people who led the American Revolution believed that the purpose of government was to serve the people, not the reverse. They rejected rule by monarchs and created in its place a **republic**. The founders of the republic later wrote a **constitution** that set up this form of government and guaranteed people's basic rights, including the right to speak their minds and the freedom to worship as they wished.

The ideals on which the United States of America was founded have inspired people all around the world ever since. Within a few years of the American Revolution, the people of France had risen up against their monarchy. Over time, the people of colonies in Central

*The **Treaty** of Alliance with France, signed in 1778, was the first military treaty signed by the new United States of America. The two nations agreed that neither of them would make peace with Britain until the British recognized the United States as independent.*

and South America, in Asia, and in Africa followed the U.S. example and rebelled against their position as colonists. Many former colonies have become independent nations.

The War Drags On

Even before declaring independence in 1776, the **Patriots** had sought help from France, Britain's long-time rival. A decisive American victory in the Battle of Saratoga in 1777 convinced the French to recognize the United States and openly to aid the Americans. In the middle of 1778, France declared its own war on Britain. Britain now had to face not only the makeshift American forces, but also the professional army and strong **fleet** of another European power.

By mid–1778, the American Revolution had dragged on for more than three years. The British had won several victories and were occupying both Philadelphia and New York City,

the two biggest U.S. cities. The Patriots, however, had performed well at the Battle of Monmouth in June. That battle would prove to be the last significant battle in the northern states. In 1778, British generals began to look to the South, where the presence of substantial numbers of **Loyalists** gave them hope that they could regain control of the former colonies.

Moment of Decision

"The present moment will decide American independence. . . . The liberties of America and the honour of the Allied Armies are in our hands."

Patriot military leader George Washington before the Battle of Yorktown, the decisive Revolutionary battle in the South, September 30, 1781

CHAPTER ONE

The British in 1778

The French alliance with the Americans worried the British greatly. One reason, of course, was that the Americans grew stronger with French aid. Another was that the British now had to worry about danger to their other colonies.

The Colonies of the West Indies

The British knew that France would attack their colonies in the West Indies. These islands of the Caribbean generated large amounts of income for the British from their sugar crops. Losing this **economic** resource would be a worse blow than losing colonies on the North American mainland.

The British, however, saw an opportunity for themselves in the West Indies. If they could capture the French islands there—France was also a colonial power, with territory in the West Indies—they would gain a larger share of the sugar trade. That would generate more income for the government and cover the expense of the war against the rebellious Americans.

The Sugar Islands

"The sugar islands are the best and surest markets for our staple commodities, and the most productive of all our colonies. They are the easiest source of our revenues."

Captain Sir Charles Middleton
of the British navy

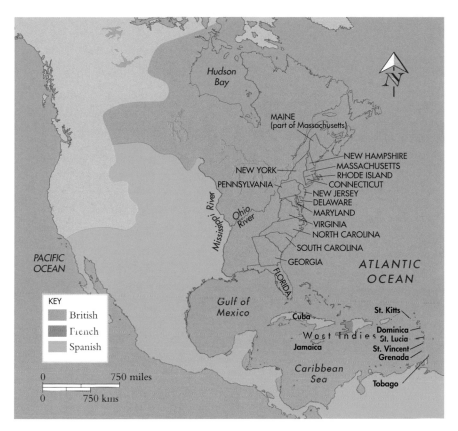

Since the 1600s, European powers had made claims to territory in North America and the West Indies. France had once held great areas of main-land North America that were relinquished in 1763 to Britain and Spain. This map shows how the region was controlled after 1763.

Fighting in the West Indies

British fears that the French would move against the West Indies were well founded. Late in 1778, a French force won the surrender of the British island of Dominica. Two months later, another French fleet tried to take St. Lucia, but a British fleet arrived first and prevented its capture. The following summer, the French captured St. Vincent and Grenada. The British and French fleets maneuvered against one another during 1779 and 1780, never engaging in a full-blown battle. The French gained two more British islands—Tobago in the middle of 1781 and St. Kitts early in 1782. The two fleets finally clashed in April 1782, when the British prevented a French invasion of Jamaica. British admiral Sir George Rodney captured five French ships and the commander of the French fleet, the Comte de Grasse.

Tobacco, indigo, and rice were profitable crops produced in the southern colonies of British North America. This picture is a tobacco label from the early 1700s. It shows a tobacco planter overseeing the work of his slaves.

The British effort to take French colonies began in the spring of 1778, soon after the French–American alliance was formed. The British government sent orders to its military commanders in the Americas to dispatch a fleet of ships and five thousand soldiers to the Caribbean island of St. Lucia. Throughout the rest of the American Revolution, French and British fleets jockeyed for position, hoping they would gain an island here or protect a possession there.

The British Plan to Invade the South

Meanwhile, Britain needed a new strategy for the revolution raging in its former colonies on the mainland. Their efforts in 1776 and 1777 in New York and Pennsylvania had not ended the rebellion. So in 1778, the British government decided to try invading the South.

The British chose this option for several reasons. First, southern Loyalists assured them that the rebellion was on the verge of collapse in that region. The British thought they would find large numbers of Loyalists, including slaves and Native Americans, to help them defeat the Patriots.

Divided and Exhausted

"No person informed of the divided, exhausted and debilitated condition of the revolted colonies will believe it possible to maintain the rebellion."

Loyalist William Smith, letter to British politician Frederick Howard, Earl of Carlisle, 1779

Second, the South was attractive for economic reasons. Its tobacco, rice, and indigo crops were more valuable trade goods than the products of the New England and mid-Atlantic regions. If they could gain a firm hold on the southern colonies, the British thought, it might be acceptable to let the others become independent.

In the summer of 1778, it was decided that General Sir Henry Clinton—the commander in chief of all British forces in North America— would send soldiers to take charge of the southern colonies. Once the army had defeated the Patriots, local Loyalist forces could keep any further rebellion in the South in check.

Henry Clinton (1730–1795)

Henry Clinton spent his teens in New York when his father, an admiral, served as royal governor there. On returning to England at age twenty-one, he joined the military. He was later promoted to colonel and also became a member of **Parliament**. Clinton was sent to America in 1775 at the outbreak of the Revolution, serving under two commanders, Thomas Gage and William Howe, before becoming the commander of British forces himself in 1778. Any hope of British success was hampered by Clinton's lack of resources, disagreements with the government, and poor relations with the navy and with Charles Cornwallis, his second-in-command. When the war ended, Clinton received much of the blame for the final defeat, although that was somewhat unjust. He later became governor of the British colony of Gibraltar, where he died.

CHAPTER TWO

The Conflict Moves South

The first British move into the South was to Georgia, the least populated of the American states. Late in 1778, British colonel Archibald Campbell led about 3,500 troops into the area.

In Georgia

The British landed just before Christmas near Savannah, Georgia's largest town. They easily overwhelmed the smaller Patriot force there and took the city. Soon after, more British troops arrived from Florida. Campbell led part of this expanded army inland to capture Augusta, Georgia, early in 1779.

In the fall of 1779, the Americans and their French allies tried to recapture Savannah. The mission failed completely, in part because the two armies did not cooperate.

Stalemate in New York

British commander General Clinton, holed up in New York City, could not follow up on the British success in Georgia. The government had ordered him to send many of his troops to Canada and the West Indies because of possible French attacks. With only 13,000 or so troops left, Clinton did not have enough soldiers to mount an **offensive**.

Clinton spent most of 1778 and 1779 bombarding the British government with requests for more troops and, sometimes, asking to be relieved of command. The Patriot military commander, George Washington, and his Continental army, meanwhile, were based just outside New York, at White Plains.

From late 1778 to 1781, the British concentrated their military efforts in the South. At first, British forces were successful: in 1779, they captured and held Savannah, and in 1780 they defeated the Patriots to take Charleston.

Clinton Heads South

Late in 1779, Clinton finally received some reinforcements and decided to renew the southern push. He left about 10,000 troops in New York City—enough, he reasoned, to prevent Washington from also heading south. Clinton and another 9,000 troops departed the city on ships in December 1779. Violent storms made the journey miserable, but the British

ships began reaching the southern coast in late January 1780. Clinton spent a few weeks assembling his forces and then made his move.

The Patriots Lose Charleston

Clinton's target was Charleston, South Carolina, the largest city in the lower South and an important port. The Patriots who held the city numbered fewer than 4,000, and they were vulnerable. Forts that commanded the harbor were in disrepair and had few guns. And the Americans' defenses on the city's land side—where Clinton planned to strike—were thin.

In February and March 1780, Clinton's army slowly made its way to Charleston. Throughout April, the British forces dug **trenches** closer and closer to the city, all the while exchanging **artillery** fire with the Patriots inside. The **siege** lasted for weeks, until British shelling in early May started fires in the city. The fires convinced the Americans to give up, which they did on May 12. About 2,500 **regulars** surrendered along

11

Patriot general Johann de Kalb (center, on the ground), second in command under General Horatio Gates, is wounded at the Battle of Camden in South Carolina in 1780.

with about 800 **militia**. The Patriots also had to give up large amounts of guns and ammunition. It was a terrible defeat for the Americans.

Guerrilla Warfare

From 1780 to 1782, North Carolina and South Carolina were involved in a bitter **guerrilla** war between Loyalist and Patriot units, many comprising a few hundred soldiers. Fights were fierce, and both sides acted with cruelty toward the other, burning homes and property and sometimes executing enemies. Francis Marion and Thomas Sumter were among the most successful Patriot leaders in this type of guerilla fighting. The best commander on the British side was Banastre Tarleton. He commanded the British Legion, a Loyalist force that at times included British regiments.

Francis Marion (1732–1795)

Francis Marion had served in the colonial militia fighting Native Americans before the Revolution. He bravely led a successful attack in his first action, gaining a name for heroism and skill. A firm Patriot, Marion helped oust the royal governor of South Carolina in 1775 and helped defend Charleston from a British attack the following year. He became a colonel and was given command of one of the state's militia regiments. Marion took part in the fights in Savannah in 1779 and Charleston in 1780. He escaped before the Patriot forces in Charleston surrendered and soon began his career as a guerrilla fighter. Marion's ability to escape into the wetlands of South Carolina earned him the nickname the "Swamp Fox." After the war, Marion served in the South Carolina state legislature.

Cornwallis Takes Charge

After his victory in Charleston, Clinton put General Charles Cornwallis in charge of British forces in the South and returned to New York. Cornwallis hoped to bring order to South Carolina. He set up **outposts** at several spots in the western part of the state.

The Battle of Camden

The Continental army, meanwhile, was on the way. By late July 1780, General Horatio Gates had a force of about 1,400 troops in southern North Carolina. But what Gates called his "Grand Army" was weary from many weeks of marching and hungry from meager food supplies. Nevertheless, after local militia arrived to support his troops, Gates ordered an attack on British troops at Camden, South Carolina, on August 16, 1780.

Panic under Fire

"The impetuosity with which [the British] advanced, firing and huzzaing, threw the whole body of the militia into such a panic that they . . . threw down their loaded arms and fled. . . . A great majority of the militia (at least two thirds of the army) fled without firing a shot."

Patriot colonel Otho Williams, describing what he saw at the Battle of Camden, 1780

Gates's Disgrace

General Gates became the object of much scorn when he fled from the Battle of Camden ahead of his men. He raced his horse for 60 miles (97 kilometers) in just one day to reach the town of Charlotte, North Carolina. After resting overnight, Gates continued riding hard. Two days later he had gone another 120 miles (193 km). He said he was seeking a place where the remnants of his army could reassemble. Some soldiers accepted this explanation. Many, however, agreed with Patriot officer Alexander Hamilton, who wrote that Gates's flight "disgraces the general and the soldier."

Horatio Gates

Gates had not prepared his attack well, however. A strong British counterattack broke the militia lines, causing the men to flee. The Continental regulars fought well but were also forced to pull back. In the disaster, over half the Continental army soldiers were killed, wounded, or captured. The militia simply returned to their homes.

The Patriots Bounce Back

Appalled at Gates's performance, the Continental **Congress**—which had put Gates in command—asked George Washington to name a replacement to lead Patriots in the South. Washington chose General Nathanael Greene, in whom he had confidence. Greene hurried south with more soldiers.

Before Greene arrived, the Patriots won two victories. The first took place at King's Mountain in northwestern South Carolina on October 7, 1780. Patriot troops had fewer than 100 **casualties**. The Loyalists they fought had more than 150 killed, an

The Loyalist troops at King's Mountain were led by Patrick Ferguson, a much-respected British major and inventor of a new, fast-firing rifle that was used during the Revolution. Ferguson was killed and buried at King's Mountain, where his grave is now within the national park that preserves the battlefield.

equal number seriously wounded, and about 700 men taken prisoner.

Fighting at Cowpens

King's Mountain was followed in January 1781 by another Patriot victory in South Carolina. General Daniel Morgan, leading a force of regulars and militia, clashed with Banastre Tarleton's British Legion at a place called Cowpens. Morgan positioned his troops intelligently and led them masterfully when their lines began to break up after a British attack. This time it was the British who lost order, with many surrendering and the rest retreating. The British lost 100 soldiers and had more than 800 captured at Cowpens, while the Patriot losses were fewer than 100. The two American victories revived Patriot spirits in the Carolinas.

Guilford Court House

After winning at Cowpens, Morgan headed north into North Carolina to meet Greene and join forces. Militia arrived from the Carolinas, too, swelling Greene's army.

Cornwallis and the British army sped north as well. The British and American armies met on March 15, 1781, at Guilford Court House in northern North Carolina. Greene developed a good plan, and his troops began firing on the attacking British army. The militia collapsed, however, when the British kept coming, and Greene had to retreat. Still, the Patriots had inflicted heavy losses on the British. Cornwallis suffered more than five hundred casualties out of a force of fewer than two thousand men. Cornwallis marched his army to Wilmington, North Carolina, on the

Our Victory

"The enemy got the ground the other day, but we the victory. They had the splendor, we the advantage."

Patriot leader Nathanael Greene, after the Battle at Guilford Court House in 1781

coast, where it could recover from its costly victory.

Spain Enters the War

While Clinton and Cornwallis fought Patriots in the southern states, the British faced other conflicts at their outposts along the Gulf of Mexico. Spain claimed a huge territory in North America—Louisiana—lying

Banastre Tarleton (1754–1833)

One of the most skillful British officers of the Revolution, Banastre Tarleton was also one of the youngest. He was only twenty-one when he volunteered for service in America. Tarleton served in a failed British expedition against Charleston in 1776 and in the fighting in and around New York that year. By late 1778, he had become a colonel in command of the British Legion. Tarleton became famous—and hated by Patriots—for his raids, winning the nickname "Bloody Ban." After the war, Tarleton's career declined. He served a few terms in Parliament and also had some postings in the army, but he did nothing to distinguish himself.

Banastre Tarleton (left) is beaten back by Patriot cavalry officer William Washington at the Battle of Cowpens. Tarleton barely escaped with his life, and the British were badly defeated.

west of the United States. The Spanish were reluctant to support American independence for fear of losing their claim, but they had allied themselves with the French against Britain. On June 21, 1779, Spain declared war against Britain and began attacking the British bases on the Gulf. These attacks tied up British forces there and prevented the British from sending more soldiers to fight Patriots along the Atlantic coast.

17

CHAPTER THREE

The War at Sea

T he American Revolution was primarily a land war fought in North America, but some significant action happened at sea as well. Several naval battles took place in the waters off the coast of the former colonies. Others were fought in the West Indies and even in the seas near Europe.

The British Navy

The British had a huge navy with nearly three hundred fighting ships. During the war, the navy was effective in preventing American and other ships from entering and leaving U.S. ports. In this way, it harmed the U.S. economy and limited the importation of weapons. The British navy, however, had some problems. Many of its ships were in poor condition, and the navy was short of officers and crew. In addition, when the French joined the war, the British had to devote naval resources elsewhere to protect other colonies. British naval power, anyway, was of little use in a rebellion that was being fought on land.

Forming an American Navy

In October 1775, the Congress had authorized the formation of the American Continental Navy. Washington ordered a small number of fishing vessels to be fitted out as fighting ships. His main goal at sea was to capture British supply ships— both to disrupt the stream of supplies reaching the British and to obtain those supplies for his army.

Privateers

There was a limit to what such a small navy could achieve, however. Much more effective were the

John Paul Jones became a leading Patriot naval commander during the American Revolution. In the early days of the war, Jones carried out many successful privateer raids.

privateers, privately owned ships specially fitted out for fighting. Beginning in 1776, hundreds of privateers were hired by the Congress to attack British ships. One of the most successful privateer captains was a young sailor, John Paul Jones.

Taking the *Serapis*

In 1779, Jones was given charge of an old, French merchant vessel, which he refitted as a warship with

Battling on the British Coast

In April 1778, sailing from France in the French-built *Ranger*, John Paul Jones headed to Britain. On the night of April 23, he and thirty of his crew rowed two boats into the English port of Whitehaven. They set a coal ship on fire, hoping the flames would spread to many —or all—of the two hundred or so ships anchored in port. Rain and quick action by the townspeople prevented the triumph for which Jones had hoped, and only the coal ship was destroyed. On the way back to France, Jones captured a British warship, the *Drake*. Jones's raid—the only Patriot attack on a British town during the war—sent a wave of fear across Britain and made Jones a hero to the French.

John Paul Jones's old, small Bonhomme Richard battles with a British warship, the Serapis, in September 1779. When the British surrendered, Jones abandoned his own, damaged ship and took over the Serapis.

Bringing the War Home

"What was done [at Whitehaven] is sufficient to show that not all their boasted navy can protect their own coasts, and that the scenes of distress which they have occasioned in America may soon be brought home to their own door."

John Paul Jones, 1778

forty-two guns. In honor of Benjamin Franklin and his famous publication *Poor Richard's Almanac*, Jones named the ship *Bonhomme Richard* (French for "Poor Richard").

In the *Bonhomme Richard*, Jones headed a small fleet of ships that sailed around the British Isles in search of vessels to attack. On September 23, 1779, Jones ran across the *Serapis* and another British warship escorting a fleet of supply ships. A long, fierce battle began. Asked by the British captain early in the fight if he wished to surrender, Jones uttered the defiant words: "I have not yet begun to fight!" Jones defeated the *Serapis*, but half his crew was wounded or killed, and his ship later sank because of damage done in the battle.

Later Naval Battles

Jones did not fight again in the Revolution. He carried out more voyages in search of merchant ships but was unable to capture any prizes.

Some other one-on-one naval battles did take place. In June 1780, the *Protector* defeated the British warship *Admiral Duff*. The *Protector* sailed not for the Continental navy but for Massachusetts, one of the states that had a small navy of its own.

Patriot John Barry captained the *Alliance* successfully, capturing several British ships during the war. In April 1781, for instance, the *Alliance* was attacked by two British ships, the *Mars* and the *Minerva*, but Barry forced both ships to surrender.

Assessing the Damage

During the war, the British added nearly 200 ships to their already large fleet. The Continental navy only managed to buy and build just over 50 ships, although privateers added greatly to the navy's impact. American ships did great damage to the British war effort: the Continental navy destroyed or seized nearly 200 British ships, and privateers took another 600 vessels.

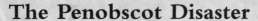

The Penobscot Disaster

One of the worst American naval defeats came in August of 1779. In June of that year, the British began building a fort at Penobscot, Maine. Massachusetts sent militia to seize it. A small fleet of three ships from the Continental navy plus other vessels were sent along to support the attack. Poor leadership produced delays and gave the British navy time to send a large and powerful fleet. When the ships appeared off the coast on August 12, the Patriot fleet scattered. The Americans ran their ships aground and burned them so they could not be seized. The Continental navy lost three of its best fighting ships, and Massachusetts lost many vessels it used to move troops and supplies.

CHAPTER FOUR

Fighting in the North and West

F rom 1779 through early 1781, the main fighting of the Revolution took place in the southern states. There was also some action on the western **frontier**, however, and in the North.

Attack in the Wyoming Valley

Fighting on the frontier was sporadic and often involved small numbers of troops. Many of these fights included Native Americans, whom the British actively recruited to join them against the Patriots.

In 1778, Major John Butler led a British effort to harass American settlers living on the frontier in the middle states of New York and Pennsylvania. Marching with a force of Loyalists and several hundred Seneca and Delaware Indians, he moved to the Wyoming Valley in northeastern Pennsylvania. Only about 360 Patriots opposed Butler's army, and on July 3 the Patriots were completely defeated. About 60 Patriots escaped. After the battle, the Native Americans attacked some of those survivors and many local settlers. Any Patriots left in the valley fled for their lives.

Cherry Valley

Later in 1778, hundreds of Loyalists and Iroquois Indians—led by Mohawk chief Joseph Brant—entered the Cherry Valley in western New York. There, on November 11, the forces attacked settlers who were supporters of the Patriot cause. The victims included women and children. In the fight, the Patriots lost about 30 soldiers and an equal number of civilians.

Early the next year, Washington dispatched a Patriot force under General John Sullivan on a revenge expedition. He ordered the soldiers to march through Iroquois lands in New York and destroy the towns there. The force carried out that work thoroughly, burning about forty Iroquois towns to the ground and destroying corn, other crops, and

The area west of the original thirteen colonies, between the Ohio and Mississippi Rivers and the Great Lakes, was known as the Northwest. The Northwest and frontier areas saw several conflicts during the American Revolution.

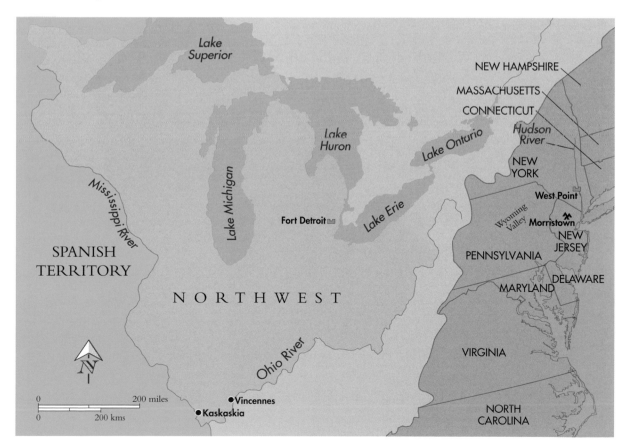

Benedict Arnold's Treason

In May of 1779, an important Patriot general, Benedict Arnold, decided to change sides. Arnold resented the fact that other commanders had been promoted over him. He was also angry over charges that he had profited from his position in the army. Arnold secretly approached General Clinton. By the time a deal was struck in 1780, Arnold was in command of the Hudson River fortress of West Point. In return for a large payment from the British, he promised to turn over the men, all equipment, and the fort.

In late September of 1780, the plan unraveled. Patriot militia captured Major John André, a British officer who had met with Arnold to finalize plans. According to Alexander Hamilton of the Continental army, "after a careful search there were found concealed in the feet of his stockings several papers of importance delivered to him by Arnold; among these were a plan of the fortifications of West Point, a memorial from the engineer on the attack and defense of the place, [and details on] the garrison, cannon and stores." While Arnold escaped to the safety of British lines, André was judged to be a spy and executed.

Benedict Arnold was paid well for his treachery and made a brigadier general in the British army. He led some British raids in Connecticut and in Virginia in 1781. After the Revolution, Arnold sailed to Britain, where he later died, deeply in debt.

John André was caught in 1780 with papers that exposed Benedict Arnold's treachery. This print shows André offering his watch to his captors in an unsuccessful attempt to win his own release.

For several months from December 1779, George Washington made his headquarters at the Ford Mansion in Morristown, New Jersey, shown here. Washington's troops were in a camp nearby.

entire orchards before they withdrew from the area in the early fall. The devastation seriously weakened the Iroquois, who were forced to rely on supplies from the British during the following winter.

Fighting in the West

Farther west, the Americans enjoyed success. A twenty-three-year-old Virginian named George Rogers Clark took about two hundred men west to gain control of the Mississippi and Ohio Rivers and isolate the main British base at Fort Detroit. Clark reached Kaskaskia, in present-day Illinois, early in July of 1778. He took over the town and other nearby settlements before capturing the larger town of Vincennes, in what is now western Indiana. Late in the year, however, while Clark was away, the British retook the town.

In February 1779, determined to get it back, Clark marched a small band of men through bitter weather and icy water to Vincennes. The British surrendered. Clark never managed to capture Fort Detroit, but he had won control of lands between the Great Lakes and the Ohio River.

Trouble in the Ranks

Throughout 1779 and 1780, General Washington had to face trouble in the ranks of the Continental army. Late in 1779, his army took up winter quarters in Morristown, New Jersey. The army suffered through brutal cold—far worse than the conditions

Poor Fellows

"Poor fellows, my heart bleeds for them, while I damn my country as void of gratitude."

Lt. Colonel Ebenezer Huntington of the Continental army, about the soldiers at Morristown winter quarters, 1779–1780

the soldiers had faced when camped at Valley Forge, Pennsylvania, in the winter of 1777–1778. Supply problems left soldiers hungry, and the Congress had no money to pay its army. The soldiers became bitter about the fact that the people for whom they were fighting apparently did so little to care for them.

The soldiers' anger increased the following spring when the country's financial problems led to widespread unrest. On May 25, 1780, two Connecticut regiments decided to leave the army and march home. Pennsylvania troops had to be called in to enforce order, and some of the leaders of the rebellious Connecticut soldiers were arrested.

Army Mutinies

A more serious mutiny took place the following year. On January 1, 1781, about 1,500 Pennsylvania soldiers left camp. They argued that their terms of enlistment—stated at "three years or during the war"—were over because three years were up. Their commanders said that the phrase "during the war" meant they were to serve until

Forty to One

The Continental dollar was a unit of exchange during the American Revolution. The dollars had been issued by the Congress to help pay for the war and as a statement of unity among the colonies. In March of 1780, the dollar was falling in value. In order to restore finances, the Congress issued a new currency. At the same time, however, it cut the value of existing currency, saying that old bills should be exchanged at a rate of forty to one. The old dollars in people's possession, therefore, were no longer worth 100 cents, but just 2.5 cents. As a result, those few soldiers who had been paid saw the value of their pay plummet.

Continental army officer Anthony Wayne (center right) tries to control a mutiny by Pennsylvania troops in 1781. During the mutiny, one officer was killed and several were wounded.

the war ended. The soldiers were also angry at the lack of pay, food, and supplies. It took several days to work out an agreement. In the end, about 1,300 soldiers were allowed to leave the service.

Resentment at conditions provoked others to take similar action.

About 100 Massachusetts soldiers marched away from camp on the same day as the Pennsylvania troops. They were seized and brought back. Later in January, about 500 New Jersey regulars walked out. They were pursued and seized as well. Two leaders of that mutiny were tried and executed.

CHAPTER FIVE

The Battle of Yorktown

While Washington was in the North, coping with problems within his army, British general Charles Cornwallis remained determined to strike a decisive blow in the South. Although the Carolinas were not yet secure, he decided to target Virginia. In April 1781, Cornwallis started to move his army there.

Gathering Forces in Virginia

The British already had a small force of just over 3,000 men in Virginia under Benedict Arnold. He had landed there in December 1780 and made some destructive raids, burning buildings and valuable tobacco crops. In late May 1781, Cornwallis arrived and took command. He had about 7,200 men, including Arnold's.

The Patriots, meanwhile, had also gathered forces in Virginia. State leaders assembled about 2,000 militia. Washington had dispatched the French general, Gilbert du Motier, the Marquis de Lafayette, from New York to Virginia with 1,200 Continental army soldiers.

The British and Patriot forces spent the next few weeks maneuvering around each other. Cornwallis tried to trap Lafayette, who was avoiding a fight until he had more men. When Anthony Wayne and 1,000 more Continental regulars arrived in June, Lafayette quickly turned to pursue Cornwallis. The British general began marching east. He had received orders from his commander General Clinton, who was at British headquarters in New York City, to seize a good port, and so he headed for the coast.

The Marquis de Lafayette was a valuable officer in Washington's Continental army. A rich French aristocrat, he also gave large sums of money to help support the American Revolution.

A Base in Yorktown

Lafayette shadowed Cornwallis along the **peninsula** between the James and York Rivers. The two forces **skirmished** at a place called Green Spring in early July 1781. The Patriots held their ground, and the British resumed their eastward move and reached Yorktown, Virginia, by August.

The port town of Yorktown sat on the south shore of the York River. Cornwallis placed most of his army around the town. He sent a detachment of troops across the river to the smaller town of Gloucester to prevent the Americans from seizing that spot and using it to attack his army.

Washington and Rochambeau Make Plans

While Cornwallis was moving in Virginia, Washington was trying to decide what to do. He had about 3,500 American troops outside New York and 4,000 French troops and a French fleet in nearby Newport, Rhode Island. Clinton, meanwhile, had about 10,500 British troops in New York. Late in May, Washington

Tired of Marching

"I am quite tired of marching about the country. . . . If we mean an offensive war in America, we must . . . bring our whole force into Virginia."

General Cornwallis, April 1781

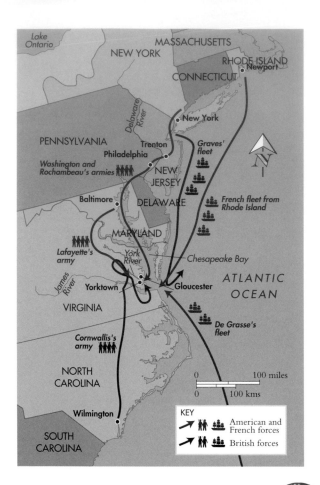

In 1781, British, French, and American forces converged on Yorktown for a decisive battle.

Marching to Virginia

"We marched 12 or 15 miles before we halted. And though the last night was so severely cold that we could not lie warm with all the clothes we had, yet after the sun rose the heat increased to that degree, together with the dust and want of water, as to render the air almost suffocating."

Continental army soldier Josiah Atkins, on the march to Virginia, 1781

Charles Cornwallis (1738–1805)

Charles Cornwallis entered the British army at seventeen years old. He served in several battles during the Seven Years' War (1756–1763) in Europe and became a colonel by the war's end. When his father died in 1762, Charles Cornwallis became the Earl Cornwallis and a member of Parliament. He opposed the government's American policies before the Revolution, but gladly went to serve in North America in 1775 with the rank of general.

Cornwallis took part in several battles in the American Revolution, including some significant defeats. Cornwallis's loss at Yorktown did not tarnish his reputation in Britain, in part because the general skillfully passed the blame onto others. After the Revolution, he served as Britain's governor general in India and in Ireland.

and Jean Baptiste de Rochambeau —commander of the French army— developed a plan to combine armies and attack Clinton's forces.

It took several weeks for the French troops to arrive from Rhode Island. Meanwhile, Washington learned of Cornwallis's operations in Virginia. Then, in mid-August 1781, he got welcome news. A French admiral—François de Grasse—was sailing from the West Indies to North America. He had nearly thirty ships and about three thousand men. Washington devised a daring scheme. He and the Comte de Rochambeau would march south to Virginia with as many men as could be spared from the New York area. De Grasse would meet them there. At the same time, the French fleet in Newport, commanded by the Comte de Barras, would bring heavy artillery for use in a siege. Cornwallis had put his army in a difficult position on the Yorktown peninsula. By surrounding Cornwallis on land and using the fleets to block an escape by sea, the allies would be in a position to destroy the British army.

A Gamble

Washington's plan was a gamble. He was not entirely confident of his men, who were frustrated and weary of war. He also could not be sure the French admirals would cooperate,

The Comte de Rochambeau was commander of the French army in North America. His good relations with George Washington and other Americans helped produce smooth operations between the two armies.

Now or Never

"We are at the end of our tether and now or never our deliverance must come."

George Washington, April 1781

although Rochambeau did his best to persuade them. And Washington could not be sure that all the forces would reach Virginia in time. But the prize—an attack on a major part of the entire British force in America—was too valuable to be ignored.

Washington and Rochambeau set out within days and moved quickly. They reached Philadelphia in late August 1781 and the Yorktown area by late September. Meanwhile, Cornwallis stayed in Yorktown, threatened by Lafayette's force nearby. The British commander believed he would receive reinforcements from Clinton, and he had no idea, at first, that Washington's army was coming south.

Digging Trenches

While Washington was marching south, Cornwallis had ordered his men to dig trenches and build **redoubts** to protect themselves against attack. He had also received encouraging news from New York. Clinton had written promising to bring more troops in early October.

Battle of the Chesapeake Capes

In early September, before Washington and Rochambeau arrived, a fierce naval battle took place. That fight—called the Battle of the Chesapeake Capes—sealed Cornwallis's fate. A British fleet of 19 ships carrying more than 1,400 guns reached the mouth of the Chesapeake Bay early on September 5, 1781. They were dismayed to find de Grasse's French fleet already there. De Grasse had 24 ships with nearly 1,800 guns.

De Grasse had to bring his ships out through a channel before he could fight, which gave the British an advantage. British Admiral Thomas Graves, however, squandered his advantage by waiting until the entire French fleet was out in the open before attacking. The two sides exchanged fire for two-and-a-half-hours before ceasing. Both fleets then stayed in the area for the next few days, each trying to decide what to do next. Both admirals were reluctant to fight again. Finally, on September 11, Graves set sail for New York, leaving Cornwallis's army to fend for itself.

The attack on the British at Yorktown began on October 9, 1781. This picture shows George Washington getting ready to fire the first cannon.

After Washington arrived, however, Cornwallis was heavily outnumbered. He had only about 7,000 men compared to the Patriots' combined American and French force of nearly 15,000. The British army was also exhausted and hungry, and many soldiers were sick.

This map shows how French and American forces managed to trap Cornwallis's army in Yorktown.

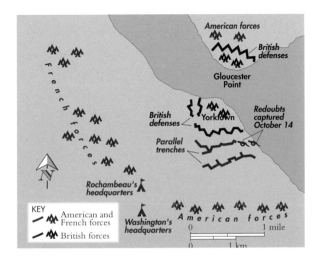

The Patriots Attack

The Patriots immediately began to dig trenches of their own in the effort to place their artillery near the British lines. On October 9, 1781, they began firing their guns from about 600 yards (550 meters) away. The bombardment continued for hours. The attack was so intense that the British had little opportunity to return fire, and many of them were injured. When heavy fire racked the British a second day, Cornwallis knew he was in serious trouble.

The allied French and Americans launched attacks on the last two British redoubts on the night of October 14, 1781. With the loss of the redoubts, the British lost their last line of defense.

Moving in

The French and Americans increased the pressure. They began digging trenches just 300 yards (275 m) from the British lines. On the night of October 14, they used these trenches to launch attacks against the two redoubts the British still held. The attack was a complete surprise. By the next morning, the Patriots had a new line of trenches with the two captured redoubts anchoring it. Early on the morning of October 16, the British attacked those trenches in an attempt to reclaim lost ground. They were soon forced to retreat.

Cornwallis had one last hope. He planned to send his army by night across the York River to Gloucester

Powerful Attack

"Against so powerful an attack, [we could] not hope to make a very long resistance."

General Cornwallis, reporting on the Battle of Yorktown, September 1781

and overwhelm the small American force positioned there. Once they had broken free, the British troops could escape north. On the night of October 16, however, a violent thunderstorm forced most of the boats carrying Cornwallis's troops to turn back to Yorktown.

Cornwallis decided he had no choice. On the afternoon of October 19, 1781, in a ceremony at Yorktown, he surrendered his force of nearly eight thousand men.

Cornwallis himself did not take part in the surrender ceremony on October 19. This print shows his second-in-command, Charles O'Hara, trying to surrender his sword to Rochambeau, who directed him to the Americans.

Too Late

General Clinton had promised to bring Cornwallis reinforcements, but he was delayed in setting out until the very day that Cornwallis surrendered. On October 19, seven thousand British troops and quantities of fresh supplies left New York City. When the ships that carried them reached the mouth of Chesapeake Bay, however, they met a small boat. People on board told them of Cornwallis's surrender, and Clinton ordered the ships back to New York.

CHAPTER SIX

The Treaty of Paris

When news of Cornwallis's surrender reached the Congress, member Elias Boudinot praised "the glorious success of allied arms." Thomas McKean, president of the Congress, thanked General Washington, calling him "the deliverer of [the] country."

Support for the War Evaporates

In Britain, the news was delivered to the prime minister Frederick North, leader of Britain's government. Lord North reportedly exclaimed, "O God! It is all over!"

Why was the Yorktown battle the final one, when there had been previous British defeats during the American Revolution? As the war had dragged on, British support for it had waned, and any remaining support disappeared quickly after Cornwallis's surrender. Shortly after the news of Yorktown arrived in 1781, a member of Parliament introduced a motion calling for an end to the war. In February 1782, Parliament

Cornwallis's Catastrophe

"What we are to do after Lord Cornwallis's catastrophe, God knows. . . . How anybody can think there is the least glimmering of hope for this nation surpasses my comprehension."

British diplomat Anthony Storer,
letter to the Earl of Carlisle, 1781

Cornwallis TAKEN !

BOSTON, (Friday) October 26, 1781.

This Morning an Exprefs arrived from Providence to HIS EXCELLENCY the GOVERNOR, with the following IMPORTANT INTELLIGENCE, viz.—

———

PROVIDENCE, Oct. 25, 1781. Three o'Clock, P. M.

This Moment an Exprefs arrived at his Honor the Deputy-Governor's; from Col. Chriftopher Olney, Commandant on Rhode-Ifland, announcing the important Intelligence of the Surrender of Lord CORNWALLIS and his Army ; an Account of which was Printed this Morning at Newport, and is as follows, viz.—

NEWPORT, October 25, 1781.

YESTERDAY Afternoon arrived in this Harbour Capt. Lovett, of the Schooner Adventure, from York River, in Chefapeak Bay, (which he left the 20th inftant,) and brought us the glorious News of the Surrender of Lord Cornwallis and his Army Prifoners of War to the allied Army, under the Command of our illuftrious General ; and the French Fleet, under the Command of His Excellency the Count de Graffe.

A Ceffation of Arms took Place on Thurfday the 18th Inftant in Confequence of Propofals from Lord CORNWALLIS for a Capitulation.—His Lordfhip propofed a Ceffation of Twenty-four Hours, but Two only were granted by His Excellency General WASHINGTON. The Articles were compleated the fame Day, and the next Day the allied Army took Poffeffion of York Town.

By this glorious Conqueft, NINE THOUSAND of the Enemy, including Seamen, fell into our Hands, with an immenfe Quantity of Warlike Stores; a Forty-Gun Ship, a Frigate, an armed Veffel, and about One Hundred Sail of Tranfports.

News of the British surrender at Yorktown spread through the new United States. This announcement of the "glorious conquest" was published in Boston.

finally voted in favor of ending the war. Lord North, worn down by the war, offered his resignation to King George III.

A New British Commander

The British prepared to negotiate peace terms with the United States and France. They also changed their

The U.S. Peace Commission

In 1781, even before the surrender at Yorktown, the Congress named five people to form a commission that would negotiate a peace treaty with Britain. One was John Adams, who had originally been charged with this task back in 1779. Another was Benjamin Franklin, already representing the United States in France. Next was John Jay of New York, who was in Spain to win that country's recognition of American independence. The fourth, Thomas Jefferson, declined the job for personal reasons. The last was Henry Laurens of South Carolina. He was in a British prison, having been captured on the way to Europe. Late in 1781, he was exchanged for Lord Cornwallis, recently captured at

Yorktown and held by the United States. Laurens traveled to Paris, France, to join the other Americans at the peace talks.

An unfinished painting shows U.S. peace commissioners (left to right) John Jay, John Adams, Benjamin Franklin, and Henry Laurens. On the far right is Franklin's grandson, William Temple Franklin.

commander in North America, replacing Clinton with Sir Guy Carleton, who had served as British governor in Canada since 1775.

Carleton arrived in New York in early May 1782 to take charge. He began pulling British troops out of other locations and gathering them in New York. In June, the British left Savannah, Georgia. In December, they vacated Charleston, South Carolina.

Negotiating the Future

In 1782, peace negotiations began in Paris, France, aiming to reach agreement about the future of North America. The chief goal of the peace commissioners who came from the United States was, naturally, full independence. They also hoped to win the Mississippi River as a western border, withdrawal of all British troops, certain fishing rights, and the freedom of Americans to move goods down the Mississippi River. The Congress instructed the commissioners to work closely with the French.

Differing Goals

Representing the British was Richard Oswald, a Scottish merchant who had lived for a while in America and who owned land in the South. He knew Laurens from before the war. His task was to make sure Britain lost no territory other than the American colonies.

A Speedy Settlement

"I really believe [Franklin] sincerely wishes for a speedy settlement, and that after the loss of dependence, we may lose no more; but on the contrary, that a cordial reconciliation may take place all over that country."

British diplomat Richard Oswald, letter to British prime minister Lord Shelburne, 1782

Representing France was the Comte de Vergennes, the French foreign minister, who had been an important figure during the American Revolution. When the war began, Vergennes had secretly funneled aid to the Patriots. After an important American victory at the Battle of Saratoga in 1777, he had urged the French king to sign a treaty with the United States.

The French had their own goals in the peace negotiations with Britain—both France and Spain did not want the peace talks to move too quickly. France still hoped to capture one of Britain's sugar islands, while Spain was planning a military expedition to seize the British island of Gibraltar.

In Europe

The first meeting between British and American diplomats took place on

April 12, 1782, when Oswald met with Franklin, the only commissioner in Paris at the time. Little of substance was discussed at first.

John Adams, meanwhile, was making political gains in the Netherlands. On April 19, 1782, the Netherlands recognized the United States as an independent nation. It also agreed to provide a badly needed loan.

As this was happening, the French received a blow to their hopes. In a naval battle in the West Indies, a British fleet had ended the French-planned invasion of Jamaica, captured some French ships, and even seized Admiral de Grasse. French dreams of gaining islands in the West Indies were ended, and France had no reason to delay further. The French were prepared to start negotiating.

At a private meeting with the French in England, the British learned that, like the Americans, France would insist on Britain recognizing U.S. independence. France, however, would be more flexible on other points. For instance, Franklin had asked Britain to hand over Canada to the United States, but the French did not make that a condition.

Recognition

Franklin and Jay—who had arrived in Paris in June 1782—grew concerned about the private talks between the French and British. At the same time, they insisted that Oswald needed a

The Fighting Goes on

Yorktown was not the last battle of the Revolutionary War. Loyalists, Patriots, Native Americans, and a few British forces continued to have small conflicts. One of the worst fights occurred in March of 1782, when over one hundred Delaware Indians, including women and children, were massacred by Patriot militia in northeastern Ohio. The militia apparently believed—probably incorrectly—that the Delaware had been responsible for a recent raid against white settlers in the area. The massacre angered Native Americans, who struck back with several raids. Patriot forces suffered defeats in the summer of 1782 in Ohio and Kentucky. In the fall, Patriot general George Rogers Clark ended the fighting by destroying several Native American towns.

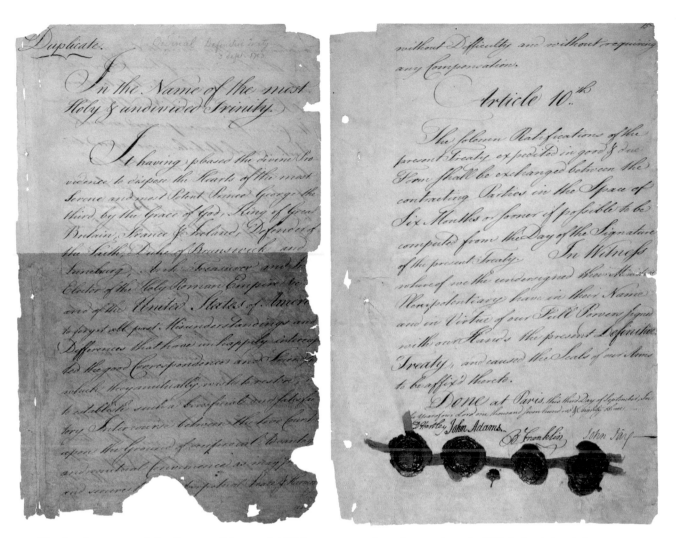

The final version of the Treaty of Paris of 1783 was signed on September 3, 1783, by John Adams, Benjamin Franklin, and John Jay (for the United States) and David Hartley, who represented Britain. These documents are the first and last pages of the treaty.

formal commission from the British government to meet with them in their roles as officials of the United States. British prime minister Lord Shelburne agreed to this step in September, indicating that Britain was already recognizing the United States. The peace talks then gained speed. Adams arrived in October. He and Jay convinced Franklin to talk to Oswald without the French being around.

The Treaty of Paris

The Americans and Oswald signed a preliminary agreement on November 30, 1782. In it, the British recognized the United States. The treaty gave the United States all territory between

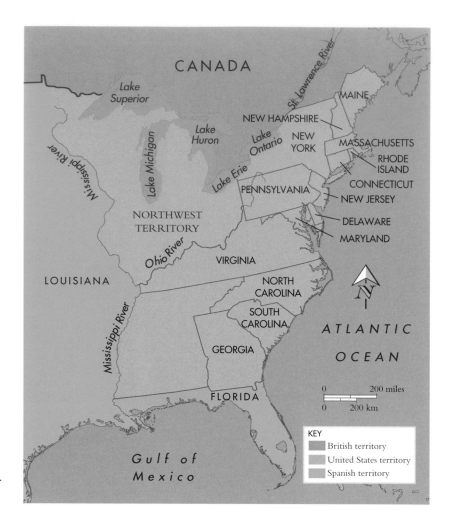

This map shows the extent of the new United States as agreed in the Treaty of Paris. The British retained Canada, where many Loyalists fled during and after the Revolution.

the Atlantic Ocean and the Mississippi River, except Florida. The British promised to pull their troops out of this territory and not to take any American property. Americans won free use of the Mississippi River, and American fishing boats kept the right to fish off the coast of Canada. The Americans promised not to block British merchants from collecting prewar debts. They also pledged to tell individual states to return property seized from Loyalists.

When Vergennes learned that an agreement had been reached without him, he was angry. But calming words from Franklin convinced the French foreign minister to bless the treaty. France and Britain signed their own preliminary agreement in January 1783. On February 4, the British officially declared that all fighting was over. The Congress followed suit in April 1783, having approved the treaty. In November, the last British forces left New York City.

Consequences for France

The American Revolution had important consequences for France. By the late 1780s, the French government was deeply in debt. A good portion of that debt resulted from French aid to the Americans. In 1789, the French government tried to raise taxes to solve its financial problems, one of the actions that led to the French Revolution— which began that same year—and the overthrow of the monarchy. Fueling that revolution were the ideals of freedom and basic rights, inspired in part by the American Revolution. The French rebels' "Declaration of the Rights of Man and Citizen" recalled the U.S. Declaration of Independence in proclaiming that "Men are born and remain free and equal in rights."

The End of the War

And so the American Revolution ended. With their bravery and determination, Americans had triumphed over the will and military forces of a powerful empire. They had united the former colonies and founded their own nation based on the ideals of equality and opportunity. And they had done this against impossible odds.

The victory, however, had come at a cost. The exact number who died is difficult to know, as records are sketchy. Some estimates say about 7,000 Patriots and about 10,000 on the British side died in battle; thousands more died of the diseases that ran rampant through the battlefields.

There was also a financial cost. The new American nation was in debt for the millions of dollars it had cost to fight the war. Individual states were several million dollars in debt as well. Those debts posed a major challenge to the new U.S. government.

Americans in Exile

Many individuals suffered physically and financially from the American Revolution. One group that suffered greatly was the Loyalists, most of whom had been born and bred in America. Like most Americans in the 1760s, they had felt proud to be part of the British Empire.

About 100,000 Loyalists left the United States. Many settled in Canada, while others went to Florida. Some chose to stay in the United States and try to rebuild their lives.

Time Line

1778   February 6: The United States and France sign treaty of alliance.
April 23: John Paul Jones raids Whitehaven, England, by ship.
July 3–4: British and Native American attacks in Wyoming Valley, Pennsylvania.
July: George Rogers Clark captures Kaskaskia and Vincennes in the West.
July 10: France declares war on Britain.
July 28–August 31: Americans and French fail to capture Newport, Rhode Island from the British.
November 11: Loyalist and Native Americans attacks on Cherry Valley, New York.
December 29: British forces capture Savannah, Georgia.

1779   January 29: British forces capture Augusta, Georgia.
February 25: Clark retakes Vincennes from the British.
June 21: Spain declares war on Britain.
August: British defeat U.S. and Massachusetts ships off Maine coast.
September 23: Jones, on the *Bonhomme Richard,* defeats the *Serapis.*
October 9–20: French and American attack on Savannah, Georgia, fails.
December 26: British forces under Clinton leave New York for the South.

1780   May 12: Patriots surrender Charleston, South Carolina.
August 16: American defeat at Camden, South Carolina.

September: Patriot militia capture John André with Patriot documents.
October 7: Patriots defeat Loyalists at King's Mountain, South Carolina.

1781   January 17: Patriots defeat British at Cowpens, South Carolina.
March 15: American defeat at Guilford Court House.
April 25: Charles Cornwallis begins marching from North Carolina into Virginia.
May 20: Cornwallis reaches Virginia and joins other British forces there.
August 20: George Washington and the Comte de Rochambeau begin marching forces from New York area to Virginia.
August 22: Cornwallis takes hold of Yorktown and Gloucester.
September 5: Battle of the Chesapeake Capes.
September 11: British ships withdraw from area of Yorktown, leaving Cornwallis abandoned.
September 28: Washington and Rochambeau reach Yorktown.
October 9: Battle of Yorktown begins.
October 19: Cornwallis's army at Yorktown surrenders.

1782   November 30: American and British peace commissioners sign preliminary peace treaty.

1783   September 3: Treaty of Paris is signed, ending the American Revolution.
November 25: British evacuate New York City.

Glossary

artillery: large heavy guns, such as cannons.

casualty: soldier or other person who is wounded, killed, or missing in battle.

colony: settlement, area, or country owned or controlled by another nation.

congress: meeting. The name "Congress" was given to the first meetings of delegates from the British colonies and was then adopted as the name of the U.S. legislature when the United States formed a national government.

constitution: document that lays down the basic rules and laws of a nation or organization.

economic: having to do with the economy, which is the system of producing and distributing goods and services.

fleet: group of ships under a single command.

frontier: edge of something known or settled. In the early years of the United States, the frontier meant the most westward point of white settlement.

guerilla: soldier or other fighter who attacks and fights alone or in a small group independently of a regular army.

Loyalist: American who rejected independence and wanted the colonies to remain British.

militia: group of citizens organized into an army (as opposed to an army of professional soldiers, or regulars).

offensive: organized attack on an enemy.

outpost: outlying settlement, such as a military post or trading post.

Parliament: British legislature.

Patriot: American who supported the American Revolution; more generally, a person who is loyal to and proud of his or her country.

peninsula: piece of land jutting out into water but connected to mainland on one side.

privateer: privately owned ship that is employed to attack enemy ships; sometimes also used to mean a sailor or captain on such a ship.

redoubt: small fortification, usually built of earth or wood, where artillery was placed to fire at an enemy.

regular: professional soldier; member of a national army.

republic: nation that is led by elected officials and that has no monarch.

siege: military operation in which a group of attackers surrounds a target and either attacks it or keeps it trapped in an attempt to force it to surrender.

skirmish: minor fight during a war or before or after a larger battle.

treaty: agreement made after negotiations among two or more nations or groups.

trench: ditch dug into the ground to protect soldiers during battle.

Further Resources

Books

Anderson, Dale. *The Battle of Yorktown* (Landmark Events in American History). World Almanac Publishing, 2005.

Gregson, Susan. R. *Benedict Arnold* (Let Freedom Ring: American Revolution Biographies). Capstone Press, 2001.

Payan, Gregory. *The Marquis de Lafayette: French Hero of the American Revolution* (The Library of American Lives and Times). PowerPlus, 2002.

Smolinski, Diane. *Land Battles of the Revolutionary War* (Americans at War: Revolutionary War). Heinemann Library, 2001.

Smolinski, Diane. *Naval Warfare of the Revolutionary War* (Americans at War: Revolutionary War). Heinemann Library, 2001.

Places to Visit

Colonial National Historic Park
National Park Service
P.O. Box 210
Yorktown, VA 23690
Telephone (757) 898-3400

Web Sites

Colonial National Historic Park
www.nps.gov/colo/
Web site of the Colonial National Historic Park, run by the National Park Service, has details about Yorktown, the battle, and historical background at the "in depth" link.

The Loyalist Pages
www.americanrevolution.org/ loyalist.html
Web site presenting the viewpoint of Loyalists during the American Revolution.

The Patriot Resource
www.patriotresource.com/history.html
Web site devoted to the history of the American Revolutionary period.

U.S. Navy – John Paul Jones
www.chinfo.navy.mil/navpalib/ traditions/html/jpjones.html
United States Navy web site has information about John Paul Jones.

Index